1

Introduction

Following the financial crisis, total outstanding loans to businesses by commercial banks dropped off substantially. Large loans outstanding began to rebound by the third quarter of 2010 and essentially returned to their previous growth trajectory while small loans outstanding continued to decline (Chart 1).[1] Furthermore, much of the drop in small business loans outstanding was evident at community banks (Chart 2). To address this perceived lack of supply of credit to small businesses, the Small Business Lending Fund (SBLF) was created as part of the 2010 Small Business Jobs Act. The fund was intended to provide community banks with low-cost funding that they could then lend to their small business customers. As of December 31, 2013, the U.S. Department of the Treasury reports that SBLF participants had increased their small business lending by $12.5 billion over their baseline numbers.[2]

In this paper we attempt to confirm the Treasury Department's estimate of the effect of the SBLF by comparing changes in the small business lending of banks that participated in the program to changes at banks that did not participate. Controlling for demographic and economic conditions that could affect the growth of small business lending, we find that banks that received funds from the SBLF increased their small business lending by about 10 percent per year more than other banks, results in line with Treasury's estimates. However, annual regressions run prior to the adoption of SBLF show that banks that later participated in the program were increasing their small business lending by about 10 percent per year more than other banks prior to the implementation of the SBLF, suggesting that SBLF participants, for the most part, continued to behave as they had prior to adoption of the program. Statistical tests indicate that adoption of the SBLF did not have a statistically significant effect on the behavior of participating lenders.

The Small Business Lending Fund

In September 2010, Congress established the SBLF. The Treasury Department set aside $30 billion to provide capital to community banks and community development loan funds (CDLFs) to encourage small business lending. Insured depository institutions were eligible to participate if they had assets of less than $10 billion.[3] Banks that had total assets of $1 billion or less were allowed to apply for SBLF funding of up to 5 percent of their risk-weighted assets. Banks with

---

[1] Bank Call Reports do not provide information on the size of the business obtaining the loan. Small loans are those with original principal amounts of less than $1 million; these loans are often taken as a proxy for lending to small businesses. These data are available on a quarterly basis since 2010, and annually prior to that.

[2] See US Department of the Treasury (2014).

[3] If the institution was controlled by a holding company, the combined assets of the holding company determined eligibility.

more than $1 billion but less than $10 billion in total assets were allowed to apply for SBLF funding of up to 3 percent of risk-weighted assets.

The SBLF also provided an option for eligible community banks to refinance preferred stock issued to the Treasury through the Capital Purchase Program (CPP) or the Community Development Capital Initiative (CDCI), under certain conditions. An institution was not eligible to participate in the SBLF if it was on the FDIC's problem bank list (or a similar list for non-banks) or had been removed from that list in the previous 90 days. Generally, this prohibition affected any bank with a composite CAMELS rating of 4 or 5.

The SBLF program was structured to encourage small business lending through a dividend or interest rate incentive structure. The initial rate payable on SBLF capital was, at most, 5 percent, and the rate fell to 1 percent if a bank's small business lending increased by 10 percent or more. Banks that increased their lending by less than 10 percent paid rates between 2 percent and 4 percent. If a bank's lending did not increase in the first two years, however, the rate increased to 7 percent. If a bank had not repaid the SBLF funding after four and a half years, the rate increased to 9 percent.

Thirty billion dollars was set aside for the program and a little over $4 billion was invested in 332 institutions through the SBLF program. This total included investments of $3.9 billion in 281 community banks and $104 million in 51 CDLFs.

The Capital Purchase Program

The CPP was launched to stabilize the financial system by providing capital to viable financial institutions of all sizes across the nation. The CPP was designed to strengthen the capital position of viable institutions of all sizes and to enable them to lend to consumers and small businesses. Unlike the SBLF, there was no explicit requirement or incentive for banks that participated in the CPP to increase their lending. At the end of the investment period for the program, Treasury had invested approximately $205 billion under the CPP. When the SBLF legislation was passed, concerns were raised that funds from the program would be used to refinance CPP loans under more favorable terms. In fact, one report estimated that $2.1 billion of the $2.7 billion lent to community banks under the SBLF that participated in Troubled Asset Relief Program (TARP) was used to repay CPP loans (SIGTARP 13-002).

Previous Literature

Six previous papers examine the effect of the CPP (or TARP more generally) on lending volumes. Contessi and Francis (2011) measure the effect of the CPP on four types of loans: total loans, real estate loans, commercial and industrial (C&I) loans, and consumer loans. Their univariate analyses find that C&I and consumer loans do not differ between CPP and non-CPP depository institutions, but that depository institutions that received CPP funds showed less of a decline in real estate loans than other depositories. They note that their results rely on the first four quarters of data after introduction of the CPP and therefore should be considered preliminary.

Cole (2012) is similar to the Contessi and Francis paper in that it studies the effect of TARP, specifically the CPP, on lending. Cole uses a panel regression model with both bank and year fixed effects to analyze changes in bank lending in a multivariate setting. His model finds that banks receiving capital injections from the CPP failed to increase their small-business lending; instead, they decreased their small-business lending by even more than other banks. He concludes that the CPP was largely a failure in this respect.

Duchin and Sosyura (2014) also study the CPP, using a probit regression to predict whether a mortgage loan is approved, with controls for differences in bank loan portfolios and demographic variables. They find that CPP funding did not cause banks to originate more mortgages, but caused a shift in the portfolio toward riskier loans at higher loan rates. After the CPP ended, banks receiving CPP funding were not significantly more or less likely to approve a loan.

Li (2013) estimates the effect of TARP funds on bank credit supply using a two-stage treatment-effects model. In the first stage, Li uses four instruments for TARP funding that measure the political situation of the bank. In the second stage estimations, Li finds that TARP banks increased their loan supply by 6.36 percent of total assets. Banks used about two-thirds of TARP funds to increase capital and lent out about one-third.

Bassett and Demiralp (2014) use panel data for the period 2009:Q1 to 2012:Q2 and an instrument similar to Li's, the political composition of the bank's home state's delegation to the U.S. House of Representatives, to identify the effect of the CPP on the growth rate of loans at domestic banks in the United States. Using a Generalized Method of Moments estimator, they conclude that the CPP did not lead to a statistically significant increase in the growth rate of loans.

Black and Hazelwood (2013) assess the impact of TARP on the riskiness of loan originations of both large and small banks. Using an event study approach, they find that small banks that accessed TARP funds decreased their risk profiles relative to small banks that did not take advantage of TARP. They also find that the level of C&I loans by small banks receiving TARP funds exceeded that of other small banks following the capital infusions. They conclude that small banks may have been able to convert the additional capital into loans without having to lend to riskier borrowers.

In one particularly relevant paper studying a foreign experience, Riding, Madill and Haines (2007) study the Canada Small Business Financing (CSBF) program, a program analogous in many ways to the SBLF. They measure the extent to which CSBF loan guarantees provide financing that would otherwise not be available, using survey data and econometric methods developed specifically to measure the incremental effect of the program. Their approach to measuring the incremental effect is a two-stage process. In the first stage, they estimate what is, essentially, a credit-scoring model, yielding parameters of a logistic model of loan decision outcomes for a large sample of non-guaranteed loans to small businesses. The second stage of the analysis uses the resulting credit-scoring model to classify a sample of CSBF loan recipients as to whether or not the firms in the sample would have been turned down in the absence of the CSBF loan-loss sharing program. The study finds that 71 of 88 loans would have been turned down otherwise and, using Bayesian inference, gives a point estimate that 75 percent of the loans would not have been made in the absence of the CSBF, with a 95 percent confidence interval of 66-84 percent.

Treasury's Evaluation of the Effect of the SBLF

Each quarter, the U.S. Department of the Treasury produces a report on the small business lending of participating institutions. In the July report, Treasury (2014) estimated the effect of the SBLF on small business lending by constructing a comparison group and a peer group of banks and comparing the change in lending of SBLF participants to the peer group. The comparison group was comprised of the 5,978 insured depository institutions that did not participate in the SBLF and (i) were established prior to March 31, 2009, (ii) had total assets between $7.0 million and $6.4 billion (the range of total assets for SBLF banks) as of March 31, 2011, which is the end of the first quarter prior to SBLF banks receiving funding, (iii) were located in one of the 44 states in which SBLF banks were headquartered, and (iv) reported a positive amount of business lending in the baseline period. Institutions were removed from the comparison group if they merged into another institution or closed. As of December 31, 2013, a total of 439 institutions had been removed from the initial 6,417 institutions in the comparison group for these reasons. The peer group was comprised of 466 insured depository institutions from the comparison group that shared certain size, geographic, and financial characteristics with the group of SBLF participants. For each SBLF participant bank, two peer banks were selected from the comparison group. The institutions selected were generally the two banks with the closest Texas ratios to the participant bank that were located within the same state and asset size category as the SBLF participant as of March 31, 2011 (the quarter immediately prior to Treasury's first SBLF investment). The five categories of asset size in this analysis were (i) $7 to $99 million, (ii) $100 to $249 million, (iii) $250 to $499 million, (iv) $500 to $999 million, and (v) $1.0 to $6.4 billion. The Texas ratio is used as a proxy for the financial condition of the institution, and is defined as the sum of the institution's nonperforming assets and loans 90 days or more past due divided by the sum of the institution's tangible equity and loan loss reserves. According to the April 2014 report on SBLF lending from Treasury, the median (mean)

SBLF bank increased its business lending by 34.7 (40.5) percent, while the median comparison bank increased its lending by 7.1 (11.8) and the median (mean) peer increased its lending by 9.5 (16.5) percent.

While this peer bank analysis is instructive, it does not take into account the full economic environment in which participating and non-participating bank operated. In this paper, we construct measures of economic and demographic conditions, market structure and competition and use a difference-in-differences approach both before and after implementation of the SBLF to tease out the separate effect of SBLF funding on small business lending.

Empirical Model

We conduct a difference-in-differences analysis in which we compare changes in small business lending by lending organizations that participate in SBLF with lenders that do not participate in the program. We control for economic and demographic differences in the local markets in which the lenders compete and for differences in market structure and competition. We estimate linear regressions of the change in business lending on a number of explanatory variables, including a dummy variable for participation in the SBLF program. In particular, we estimate the following model:

$$\Delta SB_{it} = \alpha + \beta SBLF_i + \gamma CPP_i + \pi BS_{it-1} + \Theta X_{it-1} + \epsilon_{it}$$

Where ΔSB_{it} is the change in small business lending by bank i between period $t\text{-}1$ and t; $SBLF_i$ is an indicator of whether or not bank i participated in the SBLF program; CPP_i is an indicator of whether or not bank i participated in the CPP program; BS_{it-1} is the size of the bank in total assets (logged); and X_{it-1} is a vector of market-level characteristics for the ith market in period $t\text{-}1$. These market characteristics include population (logged), per capita income (logged), the number of business establishments (logged), the unemployment rate, the level of concentration in the local banking market as measured by the Herfindahl-Hirschman Index (HHI), the CoreLogic House Price Index, and the fraction of the deposits in the market held by small depository institutions.

Data

The Small Business Jobs Act defined a small business loan to include certain loans of up to $10 million to businesses with up to $50 million in annual revenues. Loans were included if they were classified as commercial and industrial (C&I); as owner-occupied nonfarm, nonresidential real estate; as loans to finance agricultural production; as other loans to farmers; or as loans secured by farmland. Because banks that did not participate in the SBLF do not file information on small business lending that aligns perfectly with the SBLF definition of small business lending in their Reports of Condition and Income (the Call Report), we consider two measures of small business lending that can be constructed from Call Report data in our analysis. The first, more conservative measure, "Small Loans 1," is the sum of loans for owner-occupied nonresidential property; agricultural production under 500 thousand dollars; C&I loans under 1 million dollars; and farmland under 500 thousand dollars. When we compare this measure to total small business lending reported in Quarterly Supplemental Reports submitted to the Treasury by SBLF participants, we find that it is highly correlated, but consistently lower (Chart 3).[4] The second, more liberal measure we consider, "Small Loans 2," is the sum of loans for owner-occupied nonresidential property (same as above); *all* agricultural production; *all* C&I lending; and *all* lending secured by farmland.[5] This second measure is also highly correlated with the numbers reported to Treasury, but consistently higher (Chart 4).

Our sample covers the period from 2006 through 2013 and is restricted to community banks. We define a community bank as a bank or thrift that (i) belongs to a banking organization with less than $10 billion in total banking assets, and (ii) derives at least 70 percent of its deposits from a single local banking market. The latter condition allows us to tie the bank to a particular local market, and to assume that conditions in that market are likely to affect the bank's performance. Markets are defined as Metropolitan Statistical Areas or rural counties, using the 1999 definition for Metropolitan Statistical Areas. Banks less than two years old are dropped from the sample, because *de novo* banks generally have atypical levels of profits, capital and other characteristics.

Bank size and other balance sheet data come from the financial reports that banks and thrifts file with federal regulators. Demographic data come from the U.S. Census Bureau, and unemployment data come from the Bureau of Labor Statistics. Data on the number of business establishments are from the Census County Business Patterns. The HHI and the percentage of market deposits held by community banks other than the observed bank are calculated from the Federal Deposit Insurance Corporation's Summary of Deposits and the Office of Thrift Supervision's Branch Office Survey.

---

[4] For commercial banks this corresponds to the sum of the following items from the Call Report: RCONF160, RCON5585, RCON5587, RCON5589, RCON5571, RCON5573, RCON5575, RCON5579, RCON5581, and RCON5583. For thrifts prior to March 31, 2012, the small loans data were calculated as the sum of items from the Thrift report, which are slightly different from the Call Report. Starting in 2007, we use the total owner-occupied nonresidential property loans (SVGLF292). From 2012 onward, thrifts and banks all use the same variables. Thrifts are not included in 2006.

[5] For commercial banks this corresponds to the sum of the following items from the Call Report: RCONF160, RCON1590, RCON1766, and RCON1420. For thrifts prior to March 31, 2012, small loans 2 is the sum of SVGLF292 and "Unsecured Commercial Loans, Nonmortgage" and "Commercial Loans: Secured, Other than Mortgage" (SVGL1569 and SVGL1568). From 2012 onward, thrifts and banks all use the same variables. Thrifts are not included in 2006.

Table 1 presents the mean values for each variable used in the analysis, for both SBLF participants and non-participants. In general, the banks that received money from the SBLF look similar to banks that did not, although there are small, statistically significant differences in most characteristics. Just over half of the community banks that participated in the SBLF also participated in the CPP, while only 6 percent of community banks that did not participate in the SBLF participated in the CPP.[6] The banks that received funding are generally a bit larger, as measured by their own assets, assets at the organization level and by the two measures of small business lending volume. SBLF participants also experienced substantially faster growth in business lending than non-participants. SBLF participants are more likely to be in urban areas with higher home prices, more business establishments, higher per capita income, and higher unemployment rates than non-participants. The markets where SBLF participants operate are slightly more concentrated and other small banks hold a smaller share of market deposits.

Results

We first estimate our empirical model using data from the entire sample period of 2006-2013, adding yearly dummy variables to the list of explanatory variables. We then estimate eight separate yearly regressions, conduct estimations to explore changes in bank behavior over time, and run various robustness tests.

In table 2, we present four regressions giving the results of our analysis on a pooled sample covering 2006-13. The specifications differ in whether the measure of small business lending is *Small Loans 1* or *Small Loans 2* and in the way in which participation in the SBLF program is measured. In column (1), the dependent variable is the year-over-year change in *Small Loans 1* and SBLF is a dummy variable equal to 1 if a bank ever participated in the SBLF program and equal to 0 otherwise. Column (2) is identical to (1) except that it uses the year-over-year change in *Small Loans 2* as the dependent variable. Columns (3) and (4) both use the change in *Small Loans 1* as the dependent variable, but differ in their measures of SBLF participation, with (3) using the dollar volume of outstanding SBLF loans and (4) using a dummy variable equal to 1 if a lender's current balance of SBLF loans is greater than 0, and equal to 0 otherwise.

The results consistently show a significant positive effect on lending from participation in the SBLF program. The program tends to increase lending by around 10 percent. Based on total small business lending over 2011-2013 for banks that participated in the SBLF, these coefficients suggest that the SBLF increased lending by about $9.4 billion (using *Small Loans 1* as the measure of lending) to $14.2 billion (using *Small Loans 2*), results that bracket Treasury's estimate of $12.5 billion in additional lending. Consistent with Cole's findings, participation in

---

[6] The current paper does not analyze banks' decisions to participate in the CPP, but merely uses it as a control variable.

the CPP program has an insignificant effect on bank lending when *Small Loans 1* is the dependent variable and a modest (but significant) negative effect on lending when *Small Banks 2* is the dependent variable.

Coefficients on the other explanatory variables are largely as one would expect. Small banks make more small business loans in larger markets but, controlling for market size, they make more such loans in rural markets than in urban markets. The measure of bank size has negative coefficients, showing that larger banks within our sample of relatively small banks lend less intensively to small businesses than do the smallest banks; this could be the result of SBLF's less restrictive limits on payments to banks with less than $1 billion in assets than to larger banks. Lending growth is slower in markets with higher unemployment rates. Small banks make fewer small business loans in markets where more of their competitors are other small banks that are, presumably, competing to make the same type of loans. Small business lending growth is greater in markets with more valuable real estate and lower in markets in which the banking market is more concentrated and thus, presumably, less competitive. Each of the year dummies from 2007 to 2009 is significant and positive relative to 2006. From 2010 to 2011 the year dummies are significant and negative relative to 2006 in all four specifications.

While the regressions in table 2 control for many factors that could affect the volume of small business lending by community banks, they do not control for differences in business strategy, the persistence in outstanding loans on bank balance sheets, and other factors that could cause some banks to increase their small business lending more rapidly than other banks. In table 3, we present data on yearly changes from 2006 to 2013 in small business lending by banks that participated in the SBLF and by other banks. SBLF participants increased their small business loans (measured by either *Small Loans 1* or *Small Loans 2*) at a significantly faster rate than non-participants in every year of our sample, including the 2006-2010 period before SBLF had taken effect (and, in the earlier years, before any discussion of a program such as SBLF had started).

The regressions of table 4 test the implications of table 3 in a multivariate analysis. These regressions, which are comparable to regression (1) in table 2, show that SBLF participants grew their small business loan portfolios more quickly than other banks both *before and after* the initiation of the SBLF and that the difference between the two groups of banks was significant in the three years prior to the start of the SBLF and of a magnitude comparable to the effects in the years after the formation of the SBLF. Coefficients for the control variables in these yearly regressions are comparable to, but generally less significant than, the coefficients in the larger, multi-year regressions of table 2.

We formally test for any significant effects of the SBLF on small business lending volume in table 5. We conduct a "diff-in-diff-in-diffs" regression in which we compare the difference in the rate of change in small business lending by SBLF participants and non-participants before the SBLF and after the SBLF. The SBLF was adopted in September 2010, so these regressions compare changes in loan volume in the period after 2010 to the period prior to the year of adoption. The first two columns of results show the difference in the increase in small business loans from 2010 to 2011 from the increase in small business loans from 2008 to 2009. The next two columns use the average difference in annual changes in lending over two-year periods prior to (2007-2009) and after (2010-2012) the law change, and the final columns use three years of data before and after the implementation of the SBLF. All regressions for both measures of small business lending volume show that the initiation of the SBLF (and the CPP) had an insignificant effect on the behavior of SBLF participants relative to non-participants.[7]

We have conducted several robustness checks on these results. We ran analyses including additional variables, including the Texas ratio (in an attempt to capture, to some extent, the effect of the matching process used in the U.S. Treasury (2014) study), banks' net interest margin, and bank age. While all of these variables have negative and significant coefficients in our pooled regressions, their addition to the regressions does not have a material effect on the other coefficients, including the variables measuring the effect of the SBLF and CPP.[8] We ran all regressions using two-year lags of market characteristics, rather than one-year lags, but this did not substantially change the results. We ran separate regressions for rural and urban markets and found similar results for both types of market, with slightly larger coefficients on the measure of SBLF participation in urban markets, but significant effects in both rural and urban markets in the pooled regressions. Participation in the CPP had an insignificant effect on bank lending volumes in both the rural and urban subsamples in the diff-in-diff-in-diffs regressions.

Conclusion

Banks that participated in the SBLF program expanded their small business lending at a significantly faster rate than banks that did not participate in this program. However, this differential between the two groups of banks existed well before the implementation of the SBLF, and the differential in lending growth did not increase significantly after creation of the SBLF. This suggests that the SBLF had little effect on the volume of small business lending.

These results suggest that provision of capital alone is not enough to stimulate additional small business lending. Discussions with community bankers suggest that the prospect of paying 5 percent for funds—a rate that could increase to 7 or 9 percent in subsequent years—would be

---

[7] Another way to test for differences in the relative behavior of SBLF participants and nonparticipants is through the Arellano-Bond estimation method. However, this method cannot measure the effect of SBLF participation given the measures of such participation used in regressions (1) and (2) of table 2, because those measures do not vary over time for any one bank. Arellano-Bond estimation can measure the effect of SBLF participation when that participation is measured as in equations (3) and (4) of table 2. The results from these specifications do not show an increase in small business lending as a result of the SBLF.

[8] Results are not reported here, but are available from the authors upon request.

enough to dissuade the typical community bank from participating in a program like the SBLF. These discussions and our results suggest that the SBLF was tapped primarily by community banks that felt confident that they could increase their small business lending by 10 percent or more, thereby securing stable funding at an interest rate of 1 percent. SBLF participants likely held such confidence because they were located in markets where good small business lending opportunities were plentiful and where the banks had been rapidly increasing their small business lending prior to the initiation of the SBLF.

This paper has not examined the effect of the SBLF on the riskiness of bank portfolios of small business loans, nor has it explored the net cost (positive or negative) to the Treasury of investing $3.9 billion at rates comparable to or above those received on other, short-term government securities during this period. Exploration of these questions is left to future research.

Table 1: Means and Medians of Participant and Non-Participant Banks

	SBLF Participants		Non-Participants		Differences	
	Mean	Median	Mean	Median	t-statistic	Pearson Chi2
CPP	0.52	1.00	0.06	0.00	-84.63	6,478.94
Assets	12.52	12.51	12.11	11.97	-13.97	340.22
Small Loans 1	10.64	10.79	10.11	10.19	-14.24	309.33
Small Loans 2	10.93	11.04	10.35	10.35	-15.47	360.36
Diff. in Small Loans	0.24	0.12	0.14	0.03	-7.18	261.03
Diff. in Small Loans 2	0.23	0.13	0.13	0.05	-9.05	292.49
Rural	0.25	0.00	0.49	0.00	21.02	437.95
Housing Price Index	149.91	141.88	145.92	137.83	-4.00	12.16
Business Estabs	8.11	7.90	7.38	7.12	-18.03	223.67
Unemployment Rate	7.57	7.30	6.90	6.40	-9.54	64.12
HHI 100% Thrifts	0.16	0.13	0.20	0.16	12.97	274.37
Per capita Income	40.99	39.80	37.62	36.75	-15.86	175.93
Population	13.16	13.64	12.04	11.72	-20.19	399.68
Market Share of Small Banks	59.62	54.82	68.39	77.78	12.05	72.39
Organization Assets	6.55E+05	3.18E+05	1.14E+06	1.83E+05	1.23	299.37

Notes: Calculated only from community banks with at least 70 percent of their deposits in a single market; t-statistic based on two-sample t test with equal variances; Pearson Chi2 statistic based on a nonparametric 2-sample test on the equality of medians, the reported statistic is corrected for continuity.

Table 2: Pooled regression results

	(1)	(2)	(3)	(4)
SBLF	0.0947***	0.0952***	0.0105***	0.0985***
	(0.0108)	(0.00912)	(0.00170)	(0.0155)
CPP	-0.00368	-0.0137**	-0.000407	-0.00292
	(0.00724)	(0.00607)	(0.00103)	(0.0151)
Rural	0.0186**	0.0198***	0.0175**	0.0175**
	(0.00757)	(0.00625)	(0.00757)	(0.00757)
Assets (t-1)	-0.0109***	-0.00181	-0.0110***	-0.0110***
	(0.00178)	(0.00145)	(0.00177)	(0.00177)
Population (t-1)	0.00650***	0.00613***	0.00644***	0.00644***
	(0.00239)	(0.00199)	(0.00239)	(0.00239)
Per capita income (t-1)	0.000216	0.000528*	0.000255	0.000254
	(0.000366)	(0.000305)	(0.000366)	(0.000366)
Business estabs. (t-1)	-0.00295	-0.00261	-0.00317	-0.00319
	(0.00209)	(0.00174)	(0.00209)	(0.00209)
Unemployment rate (t-1)	-0.00296**	-0.00214**	-0.00282**	-0.00285**
	(0.00116)	(0.000974)	(0.00116)	(0.00116)
Share small banks (t-1)	-0.00121***	-0.00123***	-0.00122***	-0.00122***
	(0.000127)	(0.000105)	(0.000127)	(0.000127)
House price index (t-1)	0.000819***	0.000764***	0.000830***	0.000830***
	(6.92e-05)	(5.69e-05)	(6.93e-05)	(6.93e-05)
HHI (t-1)	-0.0721***	-0.0694***	-0.0734***	-0.0736***
	(0.0247)	(0.0205)	(0.0247)	(0.0247)
2007	0.726***	0.590***	0.726***	0.726***
	(0.00885)	(0.00688)	(0.00886)	(0.00886)
2008	0.151***	0.122***	0.151***	0.151***
	(0.00857)	(0.00685)	(0.00858)	(0.00858)
2009	0.0185**	-0.0180***	0.0195**	0.0194**
	(0.00868)	(0.00698)	(0.00869)	(0.00869)
2010	-0.0209**	-0.0530***	-0.0198**	-0.0198**
	(0.00993)	(0.00806)	(0.00994)	(0.00994)
2011	-0.0518***	-0.0703***	-0.0551***	-0.0552***
	(0.0102)	(0.00833)	(0.0103)	(0.0102)
2012	-0.0114	-0.0639***	-0.0146	-0.0147
	(0.0102)	(0.00831)	(0.0102)	(0.0102)
2013	0.0158	0.0224**	0.0133	0.0132
	(0.0124)	(0.0101)	(0.0124)	(0.0124)
Constant	0.0969**	-0.00383	0.101**	0.101**
	(0.0411)	(0.0337)	(0.0410)	(0.0410)
N	34,754	37,089	34,754	34,754

Notes: The dependent variable in models 1, 3, and 4 is the year-to-year change in Small Loans; in model 2, the dependent variable is the change in Small Loans 2. SBLF is a dummy variable equal to 1 for banks that ever participated in the program in models 1 and 2, as the dollar volume of outstanding SBLF investment in model 3, and a dummy equal to 1 for banks that have an outstanding SBLF balance in model 4. Extreme values of the dependent variable are eliminated, so that estimates based on the middle 95 percent of dependent variable observations. T-statistics in parentheses. Coefficients with one, two or three stars are statistically significant at the 90, 95 or 99 percent level, respectively.

Table 3: Yearly changes in small business lending

Small Loans 1

Year	SBLF Participants		Non-Participants		Differences	
	Mean	Median	Mean	Median	t value	Chi2
2006	0.17	0.13	0.09	0.05	-2.09	10.73
2007	0.81	0.81	0.68	0.59	-2.02	15.34
2008	0.33	0.17	0.22	0.10	-2.37	4.20
2009	0.24	0.11	0.10	0.03	-3.98	21.98
2010	0.19	0.08	0.04	0.00	-4.17	38.72
2011	0.12	0.08	0.01	-0.03	-4.19	96.71
2012	0.15	0.10	0.05	-0.01	-3.32	69.77
2013	0.11	0.09	0.01	0.00	-5.56	105.71

Small Loans 2

Year	SBLF Participants		Non-Participants		Differences	
	Mean	Median	Mean	Median	t value	Chi2
2006	0.20	0.15	0.09	0.07	-3.86	18.62
2007	0.69	0.59	0.57	0.38	-2.19	41.61
2008	0.30	0.14	0.21	0.12	-2.47	8.36
2009	0.21	0.13	0.07	0.04	-5.71	35.32
2010	0.19	0.09	0.03	0.00	-6.98	71.71
2011	0.12	0.09	0.01	-0.01	-5.31	85.31
2012	0.15	0.12	0.01	0.00	-6.65	113.44
2013	0.13	0.10	0.04	0.03	-6.41	64.45

Notes: Calculated only from community banks with at least 70 percent of their deposits in a single market; t-statistic based on two-sample t test with equal variances; Pearson Chi2 statistic based on a nonparametric 2-sample test on the equality of medians, the reported statistic is corrected for continuity.

Table 4: Yearly regression results, 2006 – 2013

	2006	2007	2008	2009	2010	2011	2012	2013
SBLF	0.0546*	0.0393	0.0953**	0.0850***	0.123***	0.134***	0.0914***	0.118***
	(1.650)	(0.657)	(2.166)	(3.168)	(5.600)	(7.807)	(4.479)	(8.650)
CPP	0.0487**	-0.0519	0.0220	0.0240	-0.0197	-0.0259**	-0.0102	-0.0141
	(2.531)	(-1.426)	(0.805)	(1.326)	(-1.299)	(-2.161)	(-0.713)	(-1.432)
Rural	0.0426**	0.0331	0.0520*	0.0113	-0.00557	0.0111	0.0203	-0.0141
	(2.151)	(0.869)	(1.796)	(0.607)	(-0.350)	(0.871)	(1.335)	(-1.395)
Assets (t-1)	-0.0271***	0.160***	-0.0822***	-0.0396***	-0.0290***	-0.0153***	-0.00821**	-0.0081***
	(-5.503)	(17.25)	(-11.93)	(-9.202)	(-7.821)	(-5.123)	(-2.339)	(-3.498)
Population (t-1)	0.0107*	-0.00772	0.0236**	0.00105	0.00523	0.00554	5.58e-05	0.00287
	(1.659)	(-0.628)	(2.548)	(0.174)	(0.984)	(1.294)	(0.0109)	(0.980)
Per capita income	-2.69e-05	0.00318*	-5.48e-05	-0.000588	0.000238	3.08e-05	0.00187**	0.000644
	(-0.0240)	(1.657)	(-0.0413)	(-0.667)	(0.292)	(0.0469)	(2.552)	(1.426)
Business estabs. (t-1)	0.00378	0.000249	0.00715	0.00273	-0.00999**	-0.00270	-0.00226	-0.0081***
	(0.702)	(0.0238)	(0.907)	(0.538)	(-2.328)	(-0.755)	(-0.523)	(-2.764)
Unemployment rate (t-1)	-0.00219	0.00754	0.00674	-0.000790	-0.000663	-0.00164	-0.000795	-0.0049***
	(-0.484)	(0.822)	(0.967)	(-0.222)	(-0.332)	(-1.016)	(-0.384)	(-3.392)
Share small banks (t-1)	-0.000473	-0.0051***	-0.0014***	-0.0012***	-0.000407	-0.000216	-0.000283	-0.00259**
	(-1.410)	(-2.803)	(-3.912)	(-1.416)	(-0.332)	(-0.927)	(-0.384)	(-2.565)
House price index (t-1)	-0.000257	0.00172***	0.00065***	0.000211	0.00063***	0.00040***	0.000194	0.00028**
	(-1.568)	(6.434)	(2.992)	(1.197)	(3.542)	(2.666)	(1.096)	(2.411)
HHI (t-1)	-0.0370	-0.289**	-0.153	0.0200	-0.0106	-0.0702	-0.0211	-0.0216
	(-0.548)	(-2.284)	(-1.565)	(0.321)	(-0.188)	(-1.518)	(-0.431)	(-0.754)
Constant	0.308***	-1.216***	0.818***	0.593***	0.342***	0.121	0.0761	0.373***
	(2.846)	(-5.684)	(5.015)	(5.599)	(3.605)	(1.573)	(0.834)	(3.397)
N	3,693	3,816	4,490	4,722	4,631	4,539	4,489	4,374

Notes: The dependent variable is the year-to-year change in Small Loans 1; SBLF is a dummy variable equal to 1 for banks that ever participated in the program. Extreme values of the dependent variable are eliminated, so that estimates based on the middle 95 percent of dependent variable observations. T-statistics in parentheses. Coefficients with one, two or three stars are statistically significant at the 90, 95 or 99 percent level, respectively.

Table 5: Difference regressions

| | (2010-11) – (2008-09) | | (2010-12) – (2007-09) | | (2010-13) – 2006-09) | |
	Small Loans 1	Small Loans 2	Small Loans 1	Small Loans 2	Small Loans 1	Small Loans 2
SBLF	0.0217	0.00427	0.0204	0.0219	0.0195	0.0135
	(0.636)	(0.185)	(0.411)	(0.621)	(0.396)	(0.382)
CPP	-0.0135	0.00113	-0.0136	0.0156	-0.0405	0.000217
	(-0.585)	(0.0728)	(-0.393)	(0.642)	(-1.143)	(0.00855)
Rural	-0.00360	-0.00357	0.0182	0.000392	0.0153	0.00470
	(-0.147)	(-0.219)	(0.505)	(0.0156)	(0.429)	(0.185)
Assets (t-1)	0.0124**	0.00876**	0.0203**	0.0207***	0.0331***	0.0350***
	(2.109)	(2.264)	(2.339)	(3.472)	(3.863)	(5.852)
Population (t-1)	0.00224	0.00315	-0.00651	-0.00608	-0.0207**	-0.0258***
	(0.270)	(0.567)	(-0.534)	(-0.711)	(-1.987)	(-3.484)
Per capita income (t-1)	0.000145	0.000214	0.00206	0.000775	0.00230	0.00108
	(0.113)	(0.249)	(1.174)	(0.632)	(1.423)	(0.940)
Business estabs. (t-1)	-0.00688	-0.00861*	0.00626	0.00530	0.00132	0.00328
	(-0.994)	(-1.863)	(0.615)	(0.743)	(0.129)	(0.450)
Unemployment rate (t-1)	-0.00613**	-0.0054***	-0.00690	-0.0118***	-0.00927*	-0.0151***
	(-1.965)	(-2.586)	(-1.402)	(-3.424)	(-1.806)	(-4.143)
Share small banks (t-1)	0.000856*	0.0012***	0.00138**	0.0015***	-0.00107	0.00320
	(1.915)	(3.840)	(2.082)	(3.271)	(-0.288)	(1.280)
House price index (t-1)	5.44e-05	-0.000170	-0.000351	-0.000304	-0.000705*	-0.000426
	(0.191)	(-0.898)	(-0.842)	(-1.044)	(-1.739)	(-1.479)
HHI (t-1)	-0.0303	0.0701	0.0764	0.0686	0.0824	0.0249
	(-0.342)	(1.180)	(0.662)	(0.845)	(0.806)	(0.340)
Constant	-0.230	-0.171*	-0.401*	-0.316**	-0.109	-0.418
	(-1.545)	(-1.727)	(-1.839)	(-2.089)	(-0.269)	(-1.534)
N	4,156	4,322	3,950	4,105	3,754	3,907

Notes: The dependent variable is the year-to-year change in Small Loans 1 and Small Loans 2 for (2010 to 2011) – (2008 to 2009) in the first two columns, for (2010 to 2012) – (2007 to 2009) in the next two columns, and (2010 to 2013) – (2006 to 2009) in the final two columns; SBLF is a dummy variable equal to 1 for banks that ever participated in the program. Extreme values of the dependent variable are eliminated, so that estimates based on the middle 95 percent of dependent variable observations. T-statistics in parentheses. Coefficients with one, two or three stars are statistically significant at the 90, 95 or 99 percent level, respectively.

Chart 1: Amount Outstanding on Loans to Businesses

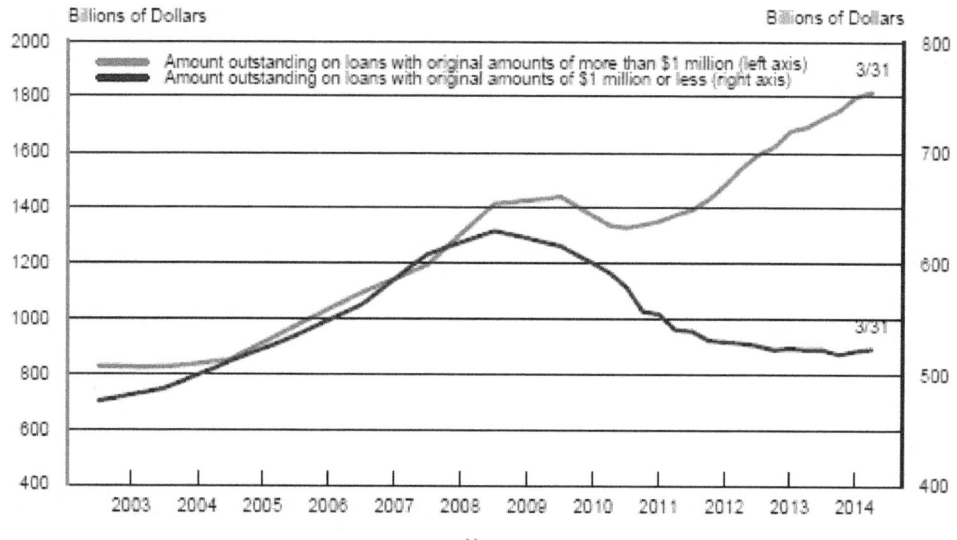

Source: These data are constructed from special tabulations of the June 30, 2002 to March 31, 2014 Call Reports (Consolidated Reports of Condition and Income for U.S. Banks).
NOTE: Beginning March 2010, the data reporting frequency changed from annual to quarterly.

Chart 2: Small C&I Loans Outstanding by Banking Organization Size

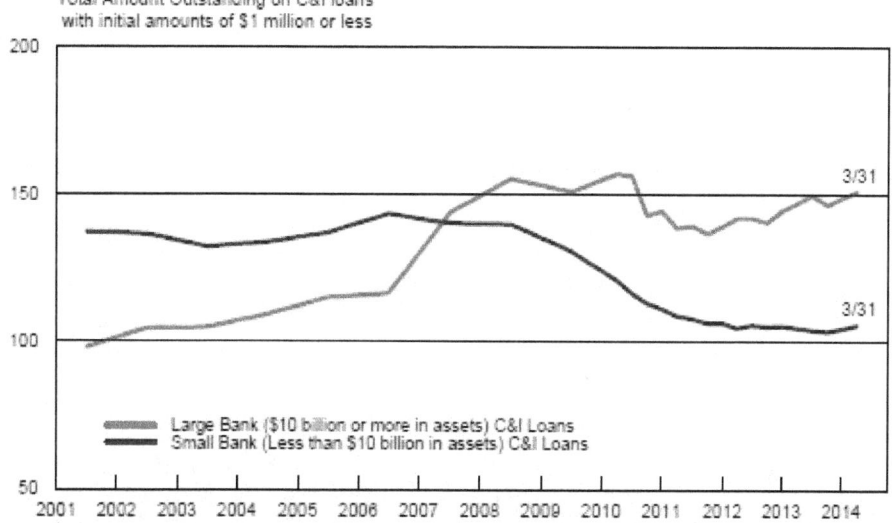

Source: These data are constructed from special tabulations of the June 30, 2002 to March 31, 2014 Call Reports (Consolidated Reports of Condition and Income for U.S. Banks).
NOTE: Beginning March 2010, the data reporting frequency changed from annual to quarterly.

Chart 3: Reported Small Business Lending to Small Loans 1

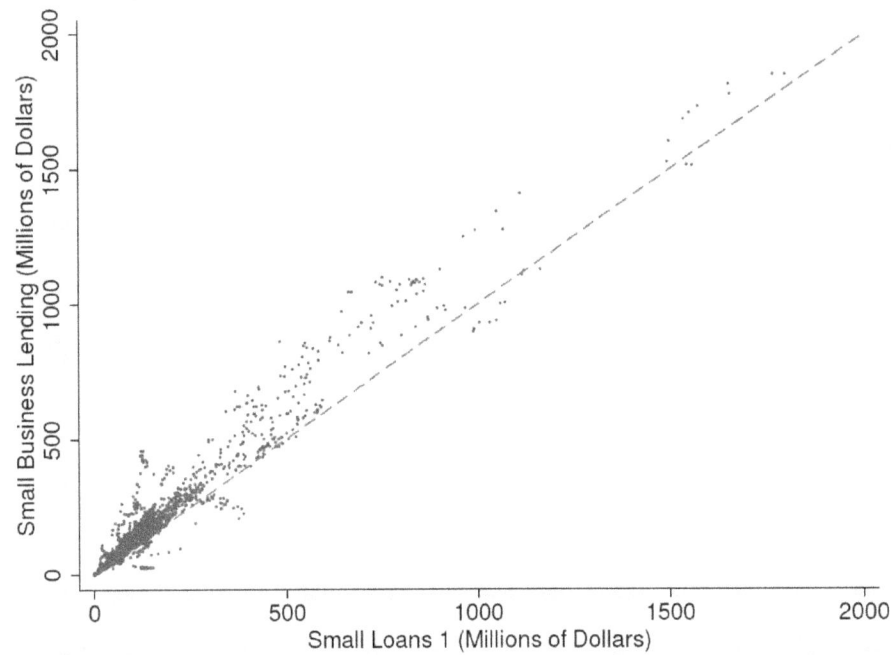

Chart 4: Reported Small Business Lending to Small Loans 2

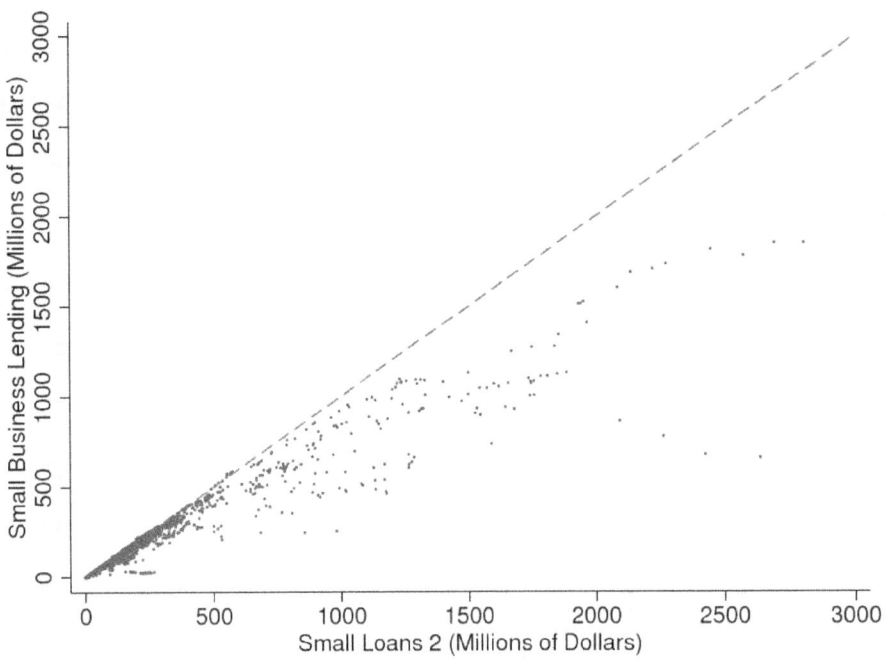

References

Bassett, William F., and Selva Demiralp. 2014. "Government Support of Banks and Bank Lending." (August 20, 2014). Available at SSRN: http://ssrn.com/abstract=2483966.

Black, Lamont K., and Lieu N. Hazelwood. 2013. "The Effect of TARP on Bank Risk-Taking." *Journal of Financial Stability* 9, no. 4: 790-803.

Cole, Rebel A. 2012. "How Did the Financial Crisis Affect Small Business Lending in the United States?" Small Business Administration Office of Advocacy Research Issue No. 399.

Contessi, Silvio, and Johanna L. Francis. 2011. "TARP Beneficiaries and Their Lending Patterns during the Financial Crisis." *Federal Reserve Bank of St. Louis Review* 93, no. 2: 105-125.

Duchin, Ran, and Denis Sosyura. 2014. "Safer Ratios, Riskier Portfolios: Banks' Response to Government Aid." *Journal of Financial Economics*, 113: 1-28.

Li, Lei. 2013. "TARP Funds Distribution and Bank Loan Supply." *Journal of Banking and Finance* 37, no. 12: 4777-92.

Riding, Allan, Judith Madill, and George, Jr. Haines. 2007. "Incrementality of SME Loan Guarantees." *Small Business Economics* 29, no. 1-2: 47-61.

Special Inspector General for the Troubled Asset Relief Program. 2013. "Banks that Used the Small Business Lending Fund to Exit TARP." SIGTARP 13-002.

US Department of the Treasury. 2014. "Report on the SBLF Participants' Small Business Lending Growth." April. http://www.treasury.gov/resource-center/sb-programs/Pages/Small-Business-Lending-Fund.aspx.

Page Intentionally Left Blank

Page Intentionally Left Blank

Page Intentionally Left Blank

Page Intentionally Left Blank

Page Intentionally Left Blank